Messages from My Heart to Yours

Monica Taylor, Author

NEWMAN SPRINGS PUBLISHING
320 Broad Street
Red Bank, NJ 07701

First originally published by Newman Springs Publishing 2023

ISBN 978-1-68498-820-4 (Paperback)
ISBN 978-1-68498-821-1 (Digital)

Printed in the United States of America

To my children, Matthew and Honi

A Promise to Love

I promise to love you always
Not as man but God unconditionally
You are my better half
For God created you for me
And all I can see is what was meant to be
There's no reason or way to let you
Slip by me this time
I've been tested, resisted, enjoyed, and enlisted
And approved with flying colors
With you telling me we're everything to each other
Honey, I can't find any other words to express how much I want to
be with you forever
You are awesome because God created you
And I'll never find another like you

September 2021

A Reminder

I've already been delivered from your mess
Passed so many tests
And continue to be blessed
As I wait for the rest
To manifest

September 2021

A True Mother

My mind wrestles with the possibility of never
Giving my children what I have wanted to for a while
As my years cut down on my chances in and maybe never seeing their
awesome smiles
I realize they already have what many don't, a mother who continues
to shower them with much love
As they realize there are so many who won't
But their Almighty Father from above

June 2021

Always Be Hopeful

Good morning!
My attitude adjustment kicked in yesterday.
Had it not, then this morning, I would have not handled several situations as well as I did.
Thanking God for his wisdom and words of encouragement daily.
I am not in any of this alone, and he continues to make me aware.
No telling what would have happened many times if I had not let him in.
So don't let a bad attitude ruin what could have been; be positive, and start over again.
Knowing God is in the midst!

August 2021

Always Ready

Ready to spread my wings and fly
Wherever I am to go before I die
Have to be patient in bursting out of here
Even though it's not my timing, let me make it clear
That this temporary space is only till I mature
And it cannot be used anymore
So I have to be ready to leap and soar
Before I die
As this beautiful butterfly

November 2021

Another Level

I've learned how to breathe
And be myself for others to truly see
As this life continues to cause me to sometimes stumble
And I find myself turning around without a mumble
To tackle what was just ahead, to live my life as the real me
Learning to love myself, to love others genuinely

November 2020

As Grown Folk

I allowed myself to fall in love with you
Allowing you to do to me what you wanted to
Why were we so afraid of getting together?
As we weathered the storms in our situation
And hearts began to tear apart on whatever with hesitation
Just didn't want to let go
Although we did know
It wasn't going to work
But had to give that love thing a try
Not knowing the real reason why
We couldn't be

March 2022

Awesome!

I cannot express my joy and gratefulness
For my Holy Spirit experiences these last few months.
My natural self has been continually excited, overwhelmed, and awed
My spirit looks forward to more of those eventful days that really
can't be explained in no other way than *Jehovah did it*!

May 2021

Because It Is Necessary

Trying, trying to make this love thing work
Shouldn't have to, but this one has a lot of quirks
To accept till they work themselves out
Guess I'll just work around them as I cry and shout
Never knew there were those who don't care about anything or any-
one other than themselves
I've learned it is difficult to show your love
When that person doesn't know how to love someone else
So I'll keep trying, trying until I get this one right
Even if I have to suffer till they see the light

May 2021

Being Over Isn't Always a Bad Thing

It's over
But all I hoped for is not dead
It's over
And it was so easy instead
The tears and yells never were
And I was able to move forward
Just because
You made it so easy

September 2021

Can't Be One-Sided

He laughs and says nothing
Watching me on the sly
Until I say something
Even if it's just goodbye
No time for childish games
Have wasted so much already
Things just aren't the same
And have never been rock steady
So now I mostly laugh with him
Because I want him to understand
That no matter what, I want to always be his friend

September 2021

Climbing My Mountains

Gonna climb this mountain
No matter how high it is
And reach the top as I hear the words of his
Gonna climb this mountain
Until it is time to be removed
And my higher level is activated
As I am spiritually approved

March 4, 2022

Endless Joy

O God
Your glory is amazing
Your love is divine
And I am so glad you saved me
In this vessel of mine
Thank you for it all
The big and small
For I am blessed even as I speak
No more or no less, you are my everything
Seven days a week!

November 2021

Every Day, God Is God Alone

Every day, God lets me see his glory
Holds me in his arms because that's where I long to be
In spite of my desire to have my man of God right here
I know it is God's will that I learn patience until he is near
No reason to rush, worry, or fear for this is in God's control
As he provides and protects my mind, body, and soul
Every day

September 2021

For Convenience

The tears are here
And the laughter is gone
Wanted to keep you near
But now want to be alone
We drifted apart even as friends
Not wanting the friendship to ever end
And when we became much more
Neither of us knew exactly what for
For the love that we seldom shared
Seemed to keep us apart
As we always tried showing each other
How much we cared
We put a wall up to guard our hearts
Finding what we needed was already there

May 2021

Forever Yours

Continuing the life we started together
Knowing there will never be another you ever
I find myself lost in someone else's arms
Full of many words and mesmerizing charm
I couldn't resist the ravishing moments allowed
And again I allowed myself to just be temporarily wowed
As I continued the life that became mine alone
I learned how to escape as into my meditation I'd roam
Finding a reason to let go
And start over to live once more

June 2021

God Always Knows Best

This is not what I was wanting
The person who likes nothing about me
But we sometimes get what we don't want
To show us just how much we don't know what we really need and
would be happy with
God knows everything; therefore, be patient
And steadfast in your trusting him
We are his children, men, and women; that will always be
Let him take care of you without being so stubborn
His plan for us is done; just wait on him

September 2021

God's Right Here

We are wading in the waters of life
Passing through the uncertainties and strife
Careful not to drown in what we don't know
As we become purified, whiter than snow
We find that each of us is special to our God
Holding onto his hand as he holds our hearts
We can never fall or fail but prevail if we do our part

December 2021

Going in Circles

O God
Don't know what's going on
But I know you do
A new friend
But don't know if the other has ended
Can only second-guess
With the situation being a big mess
O God
Help me please
To put my heart, spirit, and mind at ease
As I wait on the answers no one wants to give
And keep believing that there is a better way to live
While waiting on you

January 2021

Going Through

I'm getting quality time with my family, friends, and myself
I've learned to be content and leave the worrying to someone else
Nothing is important to most
Living nor dying
Laughing or crying
So I decided to get mine
Watching and waiting
As time takes its course
And the good and bad do their thing
While quality time is filled with a newness
Of life and songs to sing

Got to Stand

Lost in the depths of my love for him
That is truly being *in love*
Doesn't mean he feels the same way
Nor has to
I am not losing my sanity
And don't plan on it for anyone
Lost in love is enough
Got to deal with those side effects right now

November 2020

Had to Do It

By choice, I stayed
And then love got in the way
My mission was not to do all I did
But you were keeping a lot hid
Had to complete the assignments at hand
Neither you nor I was in command
Now my purpose has been made clear
By choice or not, tasks were to be done here
With love, cheerfulness, and patience
You were my test, and I couldn't get anxious
Everything happened just like it should
As we both pressed through the bad and the good

January 2022

Happy New Year

Today is only January 3, 2022
Who would have thought we would make it
So much has been said and done
Allowing ourselves to break down and take it
And take it out on everyone
But not this time as we usually say
As our hearts are searched by him in great depth and in a special way
I never understood why we rather make it hard on ourselves
Not realizing the damage we're doing and rushing our deaths

November 2020

He's Afraid

Afraid of the pain caused by someone unexpected
Afraid of the secrets that were never detected
Afraid of the love that's so loosely used
And afraid of the chance when taken being abused and misused

November 2021

How I Got Loose

Being rejected
Had not been detected
Until a minute ago
Yes, sister, I know
How much of being in denial could one be
After two and a half years of red flags being shown to me
I accepted that it was true
That the rejection was real with him not really wanting you
Not at all, while pretending to, as many things took place
I finally had to run, duck, and hide to save face
To be free
Not of him but me

February 2021

Humble Thankfulness

Healings and deliverances do come
We continue to pretend we are more than we are when we don't have
to
God treats us all equally special
Yet we selfishly want other's due
Instead of being thankful for what you already received and them too
Healings and deliverances get us through
As we learn daily what to do
Humbly

February 2021

I Continue

I continue to write
Knowing that anyone at any time could interfere with my ability to
do so
I continue to soar to parts not connected to this world for real
And understand deeper the meanings of my trials and tribulations
Communication has become almost nonexistent as we once knew
As my worrying has too
So I continue to find greatness
Which consumes every part of me
As my heart shares its every beat
Lessons of life as it exists today

September 2021

In Progress

I know you don't want to do a lot of what you're doing
And need another spiritual renewing
So take the time while you can
To become that new man
You want to be
That you'd like others to see
As you teach them how to be
That man they'll be happy to become
While teaching others in the name of love

November 2020

In Time

When the waters have run dry
And the seas are no more
We are delivered from our tears
And that which our purpose was for
As the floodgate of life
Continues to saturate our spirit
There's a new beginning with no strife
As we find ourselves embraced within it

December 2020

Joyfully

I'm joyfully on a mission that I don't know if it will ever end
As I experience many things maybe bending but never breaking
My eyes are open to the fact that this may not be what either of us
wants
Yet I find myself searching for answers
When they are usually just to taunt
I continue to joyfully do what I need to
No matter what
Even if it means I'll be the one hurt
In the end, so what?

June 2021

Just Because

We knew there was a connection
But never that it was so strong
And when it all came together
The timing seemed to be so wrong
And knowing that there is a time for everything
We chose to accept the situation as is
Receiving our many blessings
Together or not
It is what it is!

September 2021

Just on Time

Sitting in the park
Just before dark
With the birds as they pick their seats
Being fed by so many visitors
I'd look up from what I was reading with clipping scissors
In my hand periodically watching and smiling
And waiting for the storm expected later tonight
Though supposedly mildly
I want to head home to make sure everything's alright
As I enter the dark space of my living room
Preparing what I need to, first turning on a lamp to lessen the gloom
Then finishing just in time
To sit in my bay window and open the blinds
As the thunder and lightning rush my way
To help make this, as usual, another exciting, eventful day!

August 2021

Just Temporary

Here I am, Lord
Crying out to you
Having been supplied
With all I need to
Use to get through
Yet being overwhelmed at times
You are still here to ease my mind
And give me that peace surpassing
All understanding
That keeps me there until my storm is over
Stronger for whenever comes the other
In due time

September 2021

Keeping Me

My heart is flowing
Because of knowing
That I am able to soar
Soar to heights unknown by most
My confidence, cheerfulness, and boldness
Has reached a higher level of steadfastness, forgiveness, and loving-kindness
As my heart heals
Because of our God's love that's real
I don't have to be discouraged
As my spirit is kept nourished
Within my overflow

April 2021

Knowing Your Truths

I let my heart get in the middle of a great friendship
I say great, though I did question if it was even that
So many things were purposely not done
For me to see how he felt about me or us
Basically, not caring to be a couple
So I was wrong the whole time
Though his actions did flip-flop, I should have known what was going on
Next time, whether with him or not
I will not waste his or my time
True love is not difficult or problematic
It is *love*

August 2021

My Beach Experience

Out on the beach, I ran most of the night
In and out of the water until I was ready
To prepare for the rising of the sun
Had never experienced that on the horizon
My heart, my spirit, every part of me
Was in sync with the beat of the waves
And the music playing softly in the background of my location
I had one more chance to search for
Buried treasures before the amazing event
So I did, digging and digging with my hands and feet
I invited my friend as well
And surprisingly he did, but neither of us found anything, not even
a shell

November 2021

My Change Is Here

The time has come for me to do
Something more, something new
My heart can't continue crying
Being locked up feeling as if it's dying
My life has been shortened by my age already
Don't want it to be rushed because of rage but steadily
Going where it should go
Giving me and others what we should know
As wisdom brings more of what is ours
To use during the many showers
Sharing and caring like we've never before
Rejoicing in joyful songs as we open our newly given doors

December 2020

My Life's Cry

As my heart flutters
And cries tears of pain
I place myself with utterance
In a position to not lose but gain
All those things once prayed for
As my life takes turns I didn't choose
Giving me chances to open other doors
As my confidence grew
I was prepared to receive much more

My Realization

As the flowers grow
And the waters flow
My heart has been captivated
By the beauty of all that's elevated
From their existence

July 2021

Natural Beauty

In the meadows I continue to see
That which is determined to stay close to me
Nurturing and refreshing
Each day I awake and take a breath
Of its beauty and fragrance I can't explain
As each raindrop that shares my blessing
Shows their excitement each time it rains

November 2020

Nature's Way in God

I remember nature's way of taking me to places that were awesomely beautiful and peaceful
And as I experienced the presence of the Lord there, I began to write, describe, and share what his creations shared with me
I continue to keep those treasures of what God had given me in my heart, mind, and spirit as a reminder that everything given to us by God is his and he chooses to share with us because we are his as well

May 2021

Never Too Old to Learn

Somewhere, I found you in the nick of time
Without a reason to take you as mine
I didn't realize the purpose you'd be for
But now I know you were for so much more
Whether you wanted to be or not
Your destiny wasn't necessarily with me
As you thought it would be
So you were running from something that wasn't even in the plan
And now I know it wasn't for you to be my man
But for you to learn a lesson
That was actually for us both!

No Reason Not To

There's always a way to escape the enemy because we have God
There's a way to do anything we need to because God doesn't limit us
We are his, God of impossibilities
We are perfect in him; most don't know what that means
Let us believe, trust, and pray in God's will
Let's be steadfast in all he's given us to instill
In others as well!

Not Caring for Real

There's no reason to have you by my side
As I take you for a ride
For you wouldn't notice anyway
On no given day
What I'd do or say
Because you don't care
As I try to understand your moves to here
While our changes come into play
There are no reasons to want to stay
And that's what it seems you're trying to say
In so many ways

November 30, 2021

Not Just Another Day

Tonight is another chance to
Break my silence of the fear that holds me hostage
Tonight, I will make every effort to do
Not just what I need but want to
Breaking up every attempt to hinder me from living
As I wrestle with the thoughts and actions of doing my way
And staying content with things the way they are each day
Learning to please God in what I do and say always

2022

Not Our Own

Some things we probably will never understand
Especially the things we go through as humans
I've never been inquisitive as I could have been
Yet still, I have learned many lessons
I thank God for wisdom
We wouldn't be as knowledgeable as we are if it wasn't for him!

March 2021

Not Sweating It

I am so happy about our progress
And joyous for the relationship going along
My seriousness about us is still important to me
Yet there are hills we have to climb together if we are meant to be
Years or even months from now
I have faith that we're gonna make it somehow
With God in the midst, we cannot lose
This is our assignment that we didn't choose
And we are moving forward with love on our side
No matter what, we are in this for the long ride

Not the Fixers but God

What do you want me to do?
Pick myself up and leave you?
I have dedicated my life a lot
To honor and give you all I got
Yet it isn't enough
As our being together seems to stay tough
And my attempts to make you smile
Might work for a while
While I do for us, mainly for you
And you continue to do what you want to
So why don't we just do what we need to do
And that's starting over

May 2021

Nothing like Being in Love

I am in love
In love with love
Everything love stands for
Purifies my heart and renews my spirit
I am in love
Like never before
Nothing means nothing
If my heart isn't in it
For being sincere gives me so much more
As I stay in love with love and
Everything love stands for
I am so in love

November 2020

Now or Later

You'll know how much I loved you
And the many things I wanted to do
You'll realize how much we meant to each other
As time goes by as companions and lovers
And you'll finally understand why I left while
You secretly kept someone else warm
For there was someone waiting on me to share the warmth of our
new home

October 2021

Old-Time Love

Your love's the kind
That lasts throughout the end of time
The kind of love hardly no one shares anymore
One that has every good reason to live for
A love that causes time to stand still
To make even the impossible become real
Your love's the kind
That even the worst person longs to have
To experience and hold onto, to give!

September 2021

Over the Horizon

Over the horizon, there's a rainbow somewhere
As I sit on the beach with the breeze rustling simultaneously through
the sand and my hair
I am reminded of God's messages to me
To remember him who has given all I enjoy so joyfully
I then smile and cry
Wiping the tears from my eyes
To continue basking in this awesome moment
Of nature doing its thing in the midst of my sunset

August 2021

Receiving

A new day, a new song
My heart is embracing it all
With God for me who can be against me
As I steadfastly move in my position to be
Blessed abundantly as I continue to
Laugh, love, and live cheerfully!

December 2020

Right Now

We've come so far
And still have a ways to go
Yet not doing it on our own
Because we were loved and not left alone
We are a peculiar people
Different and solely made with special attention
Because we were destined for greater
As we journey toward salvation!

October 2021

Running to You, Lord

My mind says, "Let him go"
And my heart says, "Hold on some more"
Yet most of the time, I seem to know what to do
Then instead, I come running back to you
Lord, I don't want to be confused for that's not of you
So I'll just continue trying to do my best
And not forget you've already taken care of the rest
Thank you, God
For taking care of my heart!

April 2021

Sit Down Somewhere

Sometimes, we ask ourselves where did we go wrong
And other times to correct the situation
We find that we wait too long
And usually, that's our answer
For we don't take time-out to pray
Continuing to handle things ourselves
Without letting go and letting God
We just get in the way

July 2021

Staying Connected

As I drove to my destination
I began to experience a sensation
In my breathing, that was very unusual
Refreshing, uplifting, and definitely spiritual
I began to breathe in and out as if the doctor had asked me to
Can't forget thinking, *Why is this happening to you?*
Then I remembered thanking God for his breath I breathed
A thank-you that was long overdue

April 2022

Staying Me

Trying not to fret
Keeping my mind stayed on you, *Lord*
You are my present help in times of trouble
One and only true help
As I am being pulled sometimes into greater depths
You are right there as you said you would be
Doing what I can't as you take care of me
And my loved ones that you have sent me
As I try to be the best I can be
Thank you always!

January 2021

Staying on a Natural High

When meditating on the banks of the river
I recall the silence that overtook me for years
Wrapping up memories to throw into the sea of forgetfulness
As I learned to release joyous emotions into the atmosphere of remembrance
Never thought those moments of meditating would be so profound
As the river's flow changed courses while I closed my eyes and got lost in the serene sounds
That surrounded my natural highs

December 2020

Thank You, God

Thank you, God
You know how much I need you
You know how much I want to please you
Don't want to make excuses to not obey
Don't want to act like my decisions are okay
Thank you, God
For keeping me out of the way
For I don't want to mess up on any given day
Just want to listen to and trust you as I should
And be how you want me to be, and I'd hope I would

November 2020

The Experience

Flowing, soaring to the next assignment without hesitation but with
urgency and caution
Flying in mortality mode with a steadfastness
Pressing toward the final road
As joyous souls grasp onto angel wings
And nears the realm where the saints sing
I cry out *hallelujah, thank you, Jesus,* in a way I never have before
As I enter inside God's heavenly door
The first time

August 2021

The New Me

As I go to a new chapter in my life
There are things I still desire
As I push to be more assertive
I find that chances are taken to get who deserves me
And when it happens, that spark, that flame
Our hearts will never be the same
I'm not gonna fret nor faint
For God can and will do what I can't
As I move forward to better myself
Being in love with my significant other
And no one else

August 2021

The Right Move

You didn't know I wanted to ask you out
The new me is what that was all about
You avoided me after I didn't step up before
And I tried to be cool and try to ignore
You not being as forward as you were
And do what I thought was okay
But as I did, you seemed to push away
Now here I am waiting as I've learned to do
Waiting to hear you say you've been waiting on me too

January 2021

The Simple Fact

Beautiful is beautiful
On the inside and out
Wonderful is wonderful
No matter if a little or a lot
We'd rather be discontent
With all God has given
Instead of being grateful for the life we're living

June 2021

The Way I Held On

My heart has been torn
Tested by the coldness of others
Abused until weak and worn
And I refuse to allow anymore
As I walk into my destiny's door
And find the exact answers I had been looking for
While my heart is mending
And its position transcending
Into my perfect peace

August 2021

There Are Times

There are times that I am overwhelmed
There are times that rest seems slim
There are times when I want to scream
There are times when I act so mean
There are times that I just have to be still
There are times when I wonder, *Is this for real?*
There are times when I just have to say no
There are times that if I don't
Then they'll never know

October 2021

This Is How It Is

Hello
I lifted you up, and you put me down
While you didn't know, I knew you didn't want me around
But you know now it didn't matter because I have all I needed
To focus and get where I was supposed to go and avoid being mistreated
With my attitude and sanity intact
I'll never ever, not even consider, coming back
Goodbye

May 23, 2021

Time's Ticking

Don't want to waste the rest of my time here
Have made progress on certain goals, but just doesn't seem like accomplishing is near or enough
Trying to make good decisions is tough
Especially with so much this life brings
Our heavenly Father always helps
Us to do the right things
For we don't want to settle for less
But stay joyful reaching for the best

December 2020

To Give Us a Try

I will not let my heart be broken again
Nor will I break anyone's
I will protect my best friend
And work on us till we've won
No one seems to care as I do
Nor is interested enough to
So to have someone in love with me
I will allow them to show it; I'm ready

Truly Done

When this life is done
Pass the victory that's won
I hope my legacy
Will be the best of me
No games or jokes
From any unkind folks
When I am gone
I want to know that I have done
All I could, doing my part as victory is won

June 2021

Typical

A heart of a different kind
Finding ways to not connect to mine
As it wants only what it can get
Without caring or wanting this to be it
With a determined attitude of not changing its ways
Not knowing that I no longer care if it stays
I've already moved on

September 2021

Understanding Us

I do understand
Understand the love you have for me
The love you don't want anyone else to see
And the kind that's only temporary
I understand the frustration
You don't even know you have
While you stay in this situation
Along with the denial hindering us to live
Together in love

December 2021

Unstable Situation

I started feeling some kind of way
As I wondered, *Would you really stay?*
For you came out of nowhere
While I was going through then, you were there
Not stable, straight, or sure
This was a time we both had to endure
Alone

November 2020

Water of a Different Kind

Like a river flowing into reservoirs
Into the right curves and depths
Around mountains, down valleys
Through canals and caves, etc.
I find a flow that's meant to go right to you
No matter what the season
Temperature, conditions, or reason
It knows exactly what to do
As the river

July 2021

We Do It to Ourselves

Why can't we be the way we should?
When things are going bad instead of good
Why are we pushed past our limit?
When we don't even know what it is
When we are in it
There's so much to focus on these days
That we don't on God
Our concerns and worries have taken a toll
And control of our hearts
Because we let them!

November 2020

We're Not God

There are things we'll never understand
There are reasons because we are men
Men that live of the world, in the flesh
Not trying to get it, loving the mess
There are things just not allowed
For God knows what's best
And we'll never figure it out
As we continue to worry and doubt about
What he's already taken care of!

January 2021

What?

With twists, turns, and concerns
I eventually learned
That I couldn't continue in the situation
And also move in the right direction
My choice, my decision in the matter
No one else at fault as my life tatter
My will is mine given to me by God
Even if I cause myself to shatter
Into confusion, depression, and multiple sessions of prayer
With God right there
I realized it is God's will that becomes mine
And that true living in his time
Does come

2022

When We've Tried

In the midst of the storm
My friend and I kept each other warm
As we purposely didn't worry
And definitely not hurry
To get back to our "colder" homes
Full of disappointments and frustrations
Continuing to form
Honestly not knowing what to do after the storm ceased
We said only bye and to God released
Our burdens that we couldn't fix ourselves
Making a vow to stay friends while leaving our selfies on the fireplace
shelf

August 2021

You Are Our Angel

The world is a better place because you're in it
Your humbleness and kindness help you to shine more through your
meek spirit
Yes, the world is better as you spread love around it
You find time to share your blessings
And teach through them many lessons
So thank you for doing what you do
To make this a better place to live in
For we wouldn't be able to enjoy or share
our designated space we've been given

November 2021

You Got It Twisted, Baby!

No way you're gonna talk to me any kind of way
And think you'll get away with it on any given day
You are not better than me
Nor my superior from what I can see
So the drama stops here
And I am making it perfectly clear
I don't want you any more than you want me
And know I make you also sore, seemingly constantly
But we both want each other with what comes along with us
So let's be more patient and tolerable and quit the meanness and fuss

September 2021

You Will Know

You'll know when he calls regular even when you least expect
You'll know when he's affectionate toward you even with just a peck
You'll know when he says, "I miss you," and you just talked on the
phone earlier that day
You'll know when he asks several times a day
"Are you okay?"
You'll know with all of these and more
Things said and done
But most importantly, you'll just know that he's the one

May 2021

You're Better Than That

Don't let yourself fall for anything
Especially from the one you *think* loves you
They are the ones who do their best not to do
The things they know you need or give some of what you want
Believe me, don't get caught up in what you
Already know isn't going to work
You'll still hurt and feel stupid when it, whatever it is, is over
Sometimes it takes a lifetime to realize or quit, then for some a few months
We have to stop thinking less of ourselves
We are strong, wise, and patient people that
Don't have to take just anything
Remember, we have God who is with us through it all and the befores and afters
Love him first, then love yourself; he already does
And in order to get out of this cycle of being depressed, unsure, impatient, and sad
Focus on Jesus first; you'll find out that life has so much to give; let go, and let God!
In Jesus's name!

A Life Worth Living

Getting back to reality
I find that I truly love me
Whether anyone else here does or not
I am okay for I am the best I've got
As my space becomes more mine
And I get to spend in it more time
It becomes an awesome thing
As my spirit is engulfed, experiencing
Real reality at its best
While I'm not wanting to ever again have to miss
The life I've been given
By stopping truly living!

About the Author

Monica Taylor, Author was born in Gadsden, Alabama, to her parents, Mr. James K. Davis, a military veteran, and Mrs. Lula P. Davis, a dedicated homemaker. Both instilled in her to be the best she could be in life and to always love.

Monica's goals and dreams tended to always be in the caretaking fields: first nursing then day caring. Well, she didn't begin with either.

Her career took her to various jobs that she never thought of attempting, such as clothing salesperson, long-distance/directory assistant operator, deli worker, etc.

Then life's reality set in. So many ups and downs seemed to lead her right back to her first job interest, caretaking. After many years of dedication with so much support from her family and friends, helping her to be able to give her best, it was time for a change. Monica seized the opportunity, knowing it was time.

Now another journey has begun, with the new woman stepping forward to be all she can be, cheerfully!

www.ingramcontent.com/pod-product-compliance
Lightning Source LLC
LaVergne TN
LVHW091206080426
835509LV00006B/852